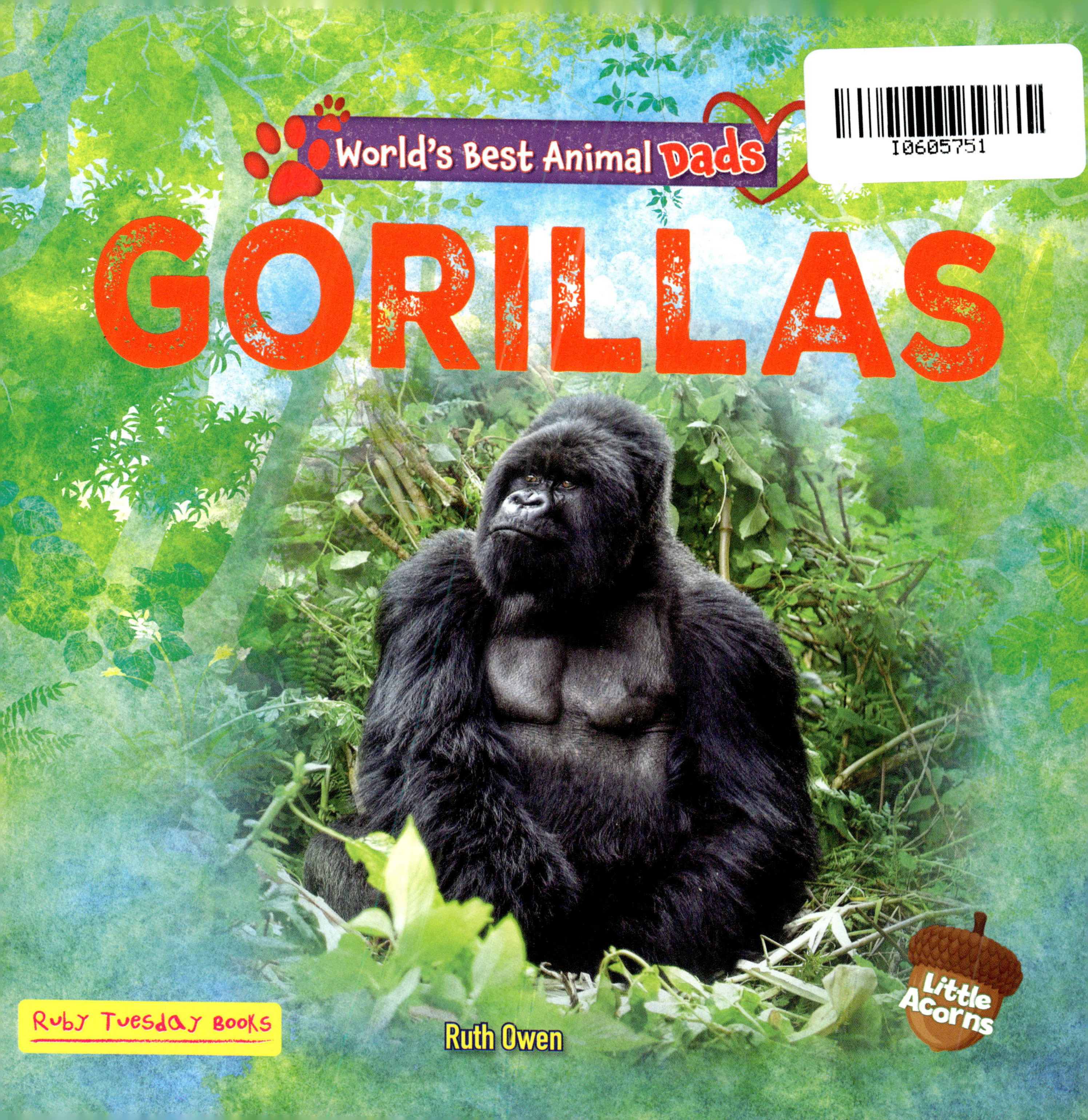
World's Best Animal Dads
GORILLAS
Ruby Tuesday Books
Ruth Owen
Little Acorns

Published in 2026 by Ruby Tuesday Books Ltd.

Editor: Mark J. Sachner
Design & Production: Tammy West

Photo Credits:
Alamy: 18 (Dimple Patel); Nature Picture Library: Cover (Suzi Eszterhas), 7 (Suzi Eszterhas/Eric Baccega), 8 (Thomas Marent), 9 (Mary McDonald), 12 (Andy Rouse), 13 (Konrad Wothe), 14 (Ingo Arndt), 15 (Andy Rouse), 16–17 (Andy Rouse), 19 (Suzi Eszterhas), 20 (Andy Rouse), 22B (Andy Rouse); Shutterstock: 4 (PhotocechCZ/Jurgens Potgieter), 5 (Gunter Nuyts/titoOnz), 6 (erwinf), 10 (AndreAnita), 11 (Onyx9/Simon Eeman), 13 (JT Platt), 21 (thisisnetnetnet), 22T (Tupungato), 23 (Wildnerdpix/Jurgen Vogt).

Library of Congress Control Number: 2025937136

Print (Hardback) ISBN 978-1-78856-597-4
Print (Paperback) ISBN 978-1-78856-598-1
ePub ISBN 978-1-78856-599-8

Published in Minneapolis, MN
Printed in the United States

www.rubytuesdaybooks.com

CONTENTS

Yawn!

A mountain gorilla family wakes up.

It's time for the big father gorilla to find breakfast for his family.

The gorillas live in a forest on a mountain.

Their forest home is in Africa.

The gorilla family has 12 members.

There are four adult female gorillas.

There are three babies and four playful, young gorillas.

The father is the dad of all the young gorillas and babies.

The father gorilla is 20 years old.

When the father gorilla was young, all his fur was black.

As he grew older, the fur on his back turned silvery-gray.

Now he is called a **silverback.**

The silverback is the leader of the family.

His first job each day is to find food.

He leads his family through the forest.

All the members of the family follow him.

The silverback finds a good place to stop.

Crunch! Crunch!

There are lots of plants to eat.

Gorillas eat **bamboo**, leaves, roots, tree bark, flowers, and fruit.

The young gorillas watch the adults to learn what tastes good.

The babies also drink milk from their moms.

Suddenly, the silverback hears a noise.

It's another big male gorilla!

The silverback makes a loud hooting noise.

Hoo Hoo

Hoo Hoo

Hooooo

He beats his chest with his huge hands.

The other gorilla wants to steal the silverback's females.

The silverback shakes tree branches.

He **charges** at the other male.

The silverback scares the other gorilla away!

A silverback's main job is to protect his family.

It's time for the gorilla family to rest.

The gorillas pick dirt and leaves from each other's fur.

This is called **grooming.**

The father makes a burping noise.

This noise tells his family, "Everything is OK."

The babies play, cuddle, and sleep with their big, gentle dad.

The silverback's little son practices beating his chest.

One day he will be a silverback.

The young male will find some females and start his own family.

Then he will also become a world's best animal dad!

Glossary

bamboo
A fast-growing type of grass with tall, thick, tough stems.

charge
To run at something, such as an enemy. An animal may charge another animal to attack it.

groom
To clean another animal's fur by picking off small pieces of dirt or even bugs.

silverback
A male gorilla that has become an adult. As male gorillas grow up, the fur on their backs turns silver.

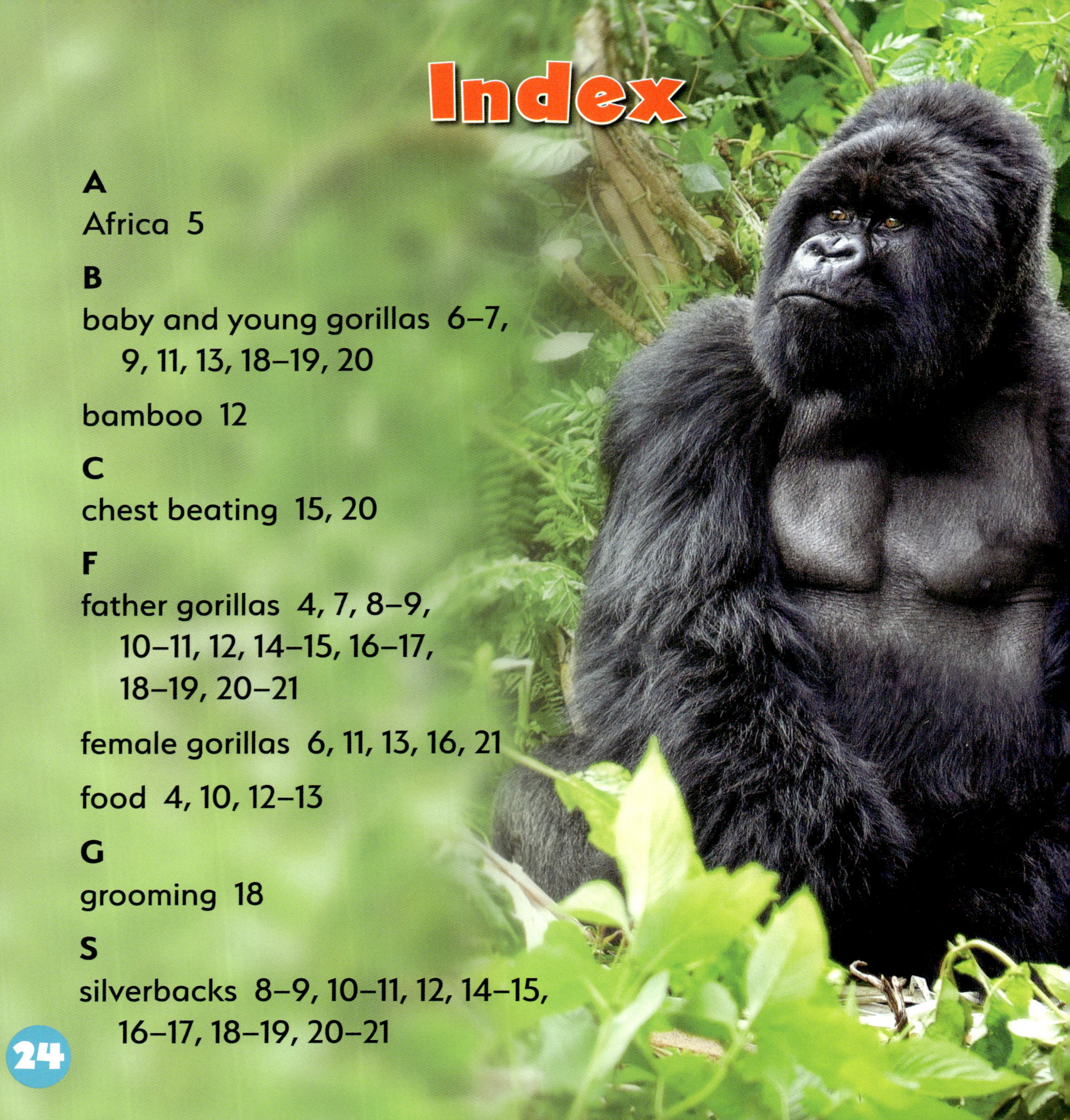

Index